Army JROTC
Leadership Education & Training
Cadet Reference

Fifth Edition

US Army Cadet Command – FT. Monroe, Virginia

D1371694

Learning Solutions

New York Boston San Francisco
London Toronto Sydney Tokyo Singapore Madrid
Mexico City Munich Paris Cape Town Hong Kong Montreal

Pearson Learning Solutions, 501 Boylston Street, Suite 900, Boston, MA 02116
A Pearson Education Company
www.pearsoned.com

Printed in the United States of America

1 2 3 4 5 6 7 8 9 10 V011 15 14 13 12 11 10

000200010270649947

RG/LP

ISBN 10: 0-558-91642-2
ISBN 13: 978-0-558-91642-8

Introduction

As a JROTC cadet you are embarking on one of the most interesting and valuable educational experiences of your high school career. In JROTC you will be given the chance to participate in your education and will learn to be a better citizen. The program provides you with tools and skills you can use to succeed in high school, but far more important, these tools and skills will b e useful for the remainder of your life.

You will learn to:

- Appreciate the ethical values that underlie good citizenship. Citizenship, taught through a study of history and government, demonstrates the importance of commitment and strengthens your character and resolve as you grow. You will learn to make ethical decisions based on core values.

- Develop leadership potential and learn to live and work cooperatively with others. Teamwork and leadership, within teams and groups, are essential to the smooth operation of any organization. You will learn leadership to increase your skills, not only to lead but to also to work as a member of a team. Service, drills, challenges, and other competitions make learning teamwork and leadership challenging and fun.

- Think logically and communicate effectively both orally and in writing. You will learn important skills in writing, reading, and test taking that will allow you to excel in your classes outside JROTC. You will learn basic problem solving, financial planning, and conflict resolution life skills that will help you live in the modern world.

- Appreciate the importance of physical fitness in maintaining good health. Fitness, wellness, and good nutrition are necessary to perform as a citizen and a leader. JROTC will teach you what needs to be done to become fit and to maintain that fitness. Instruction will be provided on how your brain functions, how you can maximize your learning and effectiveness, and how to avoid pitfalls such as substance abuse.

- Understand ways to resist negative peer pressure and support others. It is one thing to know how to make better choices for yourself and another to teach others to do the same. Through service learning you will be able to help others to develop the positive strategies you have learned that will enhance their quality of life.

- Develop mental management abilities. You will be able to assess your skills and learn to make more logical, positive decisions and choices. You will learn how to set goals and develop an action plan that will help you to achieve those goals. As you become a better citizen, a better leader, and a better team member your self-esteem will fly. Your "Can Do" attitude will show beyond JROTC.

- Become familiar with military history as it relates to America's culture and with the history, purpose, and structure of the military services. Learn not only about important events in our history, but also about their effect on our society. Discover the role the military services play in supporting the nation.

- Understand the importance of high school graduation to a success future. Develop the means and motivation to graduate from high school and to pursue a meaningful life.

- Learn about college and other advanced educational and employment opportunities and develop the skills necessary to work effectively as a member of a team. You will learn about the many varied opportunities that are available to you upon graduation. The foundation and competency skills required to work effectively are ingrained throughout the curriculum.

Table of Contents

Unit 1: Citizenship in Action... **2**

Chapter 1: Foundations of Army JROTC and Getting Involved *2*
   Lesson 3: Moving Up in Army JROTC – Rank and Structure **2**
   Lesson 4: The Signs of Success **4**
   Lesson 5: Your Personal Appearance and Uniform **5**
   Lesson 6: The Stars and Stripes **7**
   Lesson 7: Proudly We Sing - The National Anthem **9**
   Lesson 8: American Military Traditions, Customs, and Courtesies **10**
   Lesson 9: Basic Command and Staff Principles **10**

Chapter 2: Service to the Nation *11*
   Lesson 1: The Department of Defense **11**

Unit 2: Leadership Theory and Application **12**

Chapter 1: Being a Leader *12*
   Lesson 3: Leadership from the Inside Out **12**
   Lesson 4: Principles and Leadership **12**

Chapter 2: Leadership Skills *13*
   Lesson 4: Stationary Movements **13**
   Lesson 5: Steps and Marching **14**
   Lesson 6: Squad Drill **15**

Chapter 4: Leadership Strategies *17*
   Lesson 2: Performance Indicators **17**
   Lesson 4: Decision Making and Problem Solving **17**

Chapter 5: Leading Others *19*
   Lesson 1: Platoon Drill **19**
   Lesson 3: Company Formations and Movement **20**
   Lesson 4: Forming, Inspection, and Dismissing the Battalion **22**

Unit 3: Foundations for Success **24**

Chapter 1: Know Yourself - Socrates *24*
   Lesson 1: Self-Awareness **24**
   Lesson 5: Pathways to Success (QBOL) **25**

Chapter 2: Learning to Learn *26*
   Lesson 1: Brain Structure and Function **26**
   Lesson 2: Left-Brain/Right-Brain **26**

Chapter 5: Conflict Resolution *27*
   Lesson 1: Causes of Conflict **27**

Chapter 8: Making a Difference with Service Learning *28*
   Lesson 1: Orientation to Service Learning **28**
   Lesson 2: Plan and Train for Your Exploratory Project **28**

Chapter 9: Career Planning *29*
   Lesson 2: Career Development Portfolio **29**

Chapter 10: Planning Skills and Social Responsibility..30
Lesson 1: Making the Right Choices..30
Lesson 4: Cadet Etiquette Guide...30

Chapter 12: Teaching Skills 31
Lesson 5: Thinking Maps® and Graphic Organizers 31

Unit 4: Wellness, Fitness, and First Aid...34

Chapter 1: Achieving a Healthy Lifestyle...34
Lesson 2: Cadet Challenge 34
Lesson 4: Nutrition - You Are What You Eat...37
Lesson 5: At Risk - Suicide Awareness and Prevention 38

Unit 6: Citizenship and American History 39

Chapter 1: You the People – The Citizenship Skills 39
Lesson 1: The Preamble 39

Chapter 3: Creating the Constitution...39
Lesson 1: Articles of Confederation 1781 39

The Junior ROTC Cadet Creed

I am an Army Junior ROTC Cadet.

I will always conduct myself to bring credit to my family, country, school and the Corps of Cadets.

I am loyal and patriotic. I am the future of the United States of America.

I do not lie, cheat or steal and will always be accountable for my actions and deeds.

I will always practice good citizenship and patriotism.

I will work hard to improve my mind and strengthen my body.

I will seek the mantel of leadership and stand prepared to uphold the Constitution and the American way of life.

May God grant me the strength to always live by this creed.

Unit 1: Citizenship in Action
Chapter 1: Foundations of Army JROTC and Getting Involved
Lesson 3: Moving Up in Army JROTC – Rank and Structure

CATEGORY	Insignia of the United States Army					
ENLISTED (Green and Gold)	E-1	E-2	E-3	E-4		E-5	E-6

ENLISTED (Green and Gold)

E-1	E-2	E-3	E-4		E-5	E-6
no insignia Private	Private	Private 1st Class	Corporal	Specialist	Sergeant	Staff Sergeant

E-7	E-8		E-9		
Sergeant 1st Class	Master Sergeant	1st Sergeant	Sergeant Major	Command Sergeant Major	Sergeant Major of the Army

WARRANT OFFICER (Silver and Black)

W-1	W-2	W-3	W-4	W-5
Warrant Officer	Chief Warrant Officer	Chief Warrant Officer	Chief Warrant Officer	Master Warrant Officer

COMPANY AND FIELD GRADE OFFICER (Gold and Silver)

0-1	0-2	0-3	0-4	0-5	0-6
(gold) 2nd Lieutenant	(silver) 1st Lieutenant	(silver) Captain	(gold) Major	(silver) Lieutenant Colonel	(silver) Colonel

GENERAL OFFICER (Silver)

0-7	0-8	0-9	0-10	0-11
Brigadier General	Major General	Lieutenant General	General	General of the Army

INSIGNIA OF GRADE FOR CADET OFFICERS

CADET COLONEL

CADET LIEUTENANT COLONEL

CADET MAJOR

CADET CAPTAIN

CADET FIRST LIEUTENANT

CADET SECOND LIEUTENANT

INSIGNIA OF GRADE FOR CADET ENLISTED PERSONNEL

CADET COMMAND SERGEANT MAJOR

CADET SERGEANT MAJOR

CADET FIRST SERGEANT

CADET MASTER SERGEANT

CADET SERGEANT FIRST CLASS

CADET STAFF SERGEANT

CADET SERGEANT

CADET CORPORAL

CADET PRIVATE FIRST CLASS

CADET PRIVATE

Battalion Organization

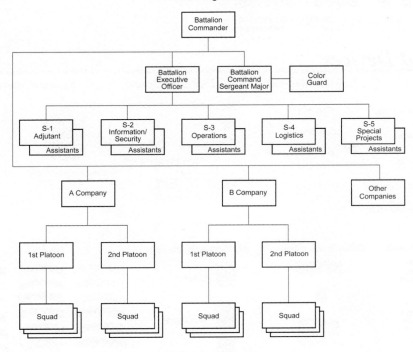

Unit 1: Citizenship in Action
Chapter 1: Foundations of Army JROTC and Getting Involved
Lesson 4: The Signs of Success

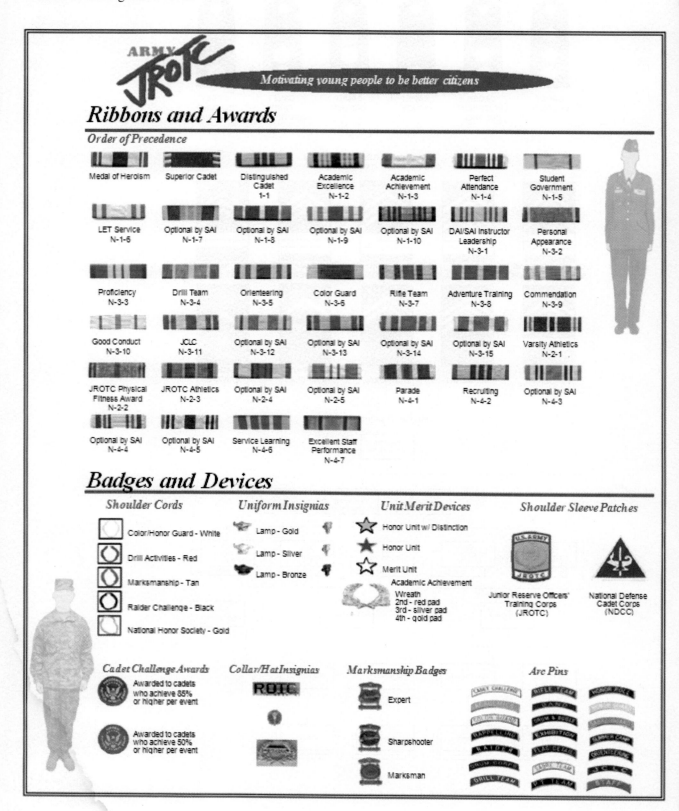

Unit 1: Citizenship in Action
Chapter 1: Foundations of Army JROTC and Getting Involved
Lesson 5: Your Personal Appearance and Uniform

ARMY JROTC

Motivating young people to be better citizens

Center rank insignia on the shoulder loop 5/8 inch from the outside shoulder seam (all cadet officers).

The unit crest will be worn centered 1/4 inch above the HU, HUD or MU or 1/4 above the nameplate (all cadets).

When worn, center Special JROTC team pins (arcs) between the bottom of the pocket flap and the bottom of the pocket. If more than one team pin is worn, space them 1/8 inch between each arch (male cadets).

Male black oxford shoes are authorized for wear (all males).

Place the ROTC insignia 5/8 inch above the notch on both collars, with the centerline of the insignia bisecting the notch and parallel to the inside edge of the lapel (male cadet officers).

Center Torch of Knowledge insignia on both lapels 1 1/4 inches below the ROTC insignia, with the centerline of the insignia bisecting the ROTC insignia and parallel to the inside edge of the lapel (all cadet officers).

Center ribbons 1/8 inch above the top of pocket flap. Third and subsequent rows may be aligned to the left to present a better appearance (all male cadets).

The rank insignia is worn centered on the garrison cap left curtain, 1 inch from the front crease (all cadet officers).

Center the name-plate horizontally on the right side between 1 and 2 inches above the top button. Adjust placement of the nameplate to conform to individual figure differences (all females).

Black oxford shoes or black service pumps may be worn. The pump will be plain, with closed toe and heel. The heel will be between 1/2 and 3 inches high (all female cadets).

Place the ROTC insignia 5/8 inch up from the collar and lapel seam with the center line of the insignia parallel to the inside edge of the lapel (female cadet officers).

Center JROTC shoulder-sleeve insignia on the left sleeve 1/2 below the top of the shoulder seam (all cadets). The school shoulder-sleeve insignia may be worn in the same fashion on the right.

When worn, place Special JROTC team pins (arcs) parallel to the waistline of the coat. Placement of the team pins may be adjusted to conform to the individual figure difference, space pins 1/8 inch between each arc (all female cadets).

THE ARMY JROTC UNIFORM

Center rank insignia epaulets on the shoulder so that the insignia will be centered on the outer half of both shoulder loops of the coat. When wearing rank disc insignia, the disc will be centered between the bottom of the button hole and the top of the shoulder seam of the garment (all enlisted cadets).

Center the HU, HUD or MU insignia 1/4 inch above the right breast pocket on the male uniform and 1/4 inch above the name-plate on the female uniform. It can be worn by itself or joined by the Academic Achievement Wreath, in which case the star is still positioned 1/4 inch above the name-plate.

The JROTC cap insignia is a wreath 1 3/16 inches in height containing the letter "ROTC" on a gold color metal panel inside the wreath. Place the insignia 1 inch from the crease on the garrison cap left curtain (all enlisted cadets).

Place the JROTC Corps insignia centered on both lapels of the coat, parallel to the inside edge of each lapel; 5/8 inch above the notch (enlisted female cadets); 1 inch above the notch (enlisted male cadets).

Center ribbons on the left side with the bottom row parallel to the bottom edge of the nameplate. Third and subsequent rows may be aligned to the left to present a better appearance (all female cadets).

Army Green Garrison Cap

Shoulder Marks

Army Green Long or Short Sleeve shirt

Black Necktie/Neck Tab (mandatory with long sleeve shirt, optional with short sleeve shirt)

Black Belt with a gold plated buckle

Army Green Slacks

Black Socks

Black Low Quarter Shoes or Pumps

Motivating young people to be better citizens

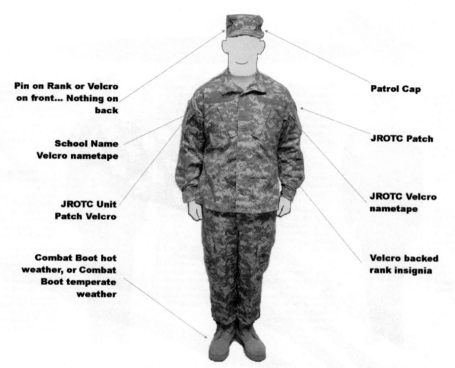

Pin on Rank or Velcro on front... Nothing on back

Patrol Cap

School Name Velcro nametape

JROTC Patch

JROTC Unit Patch Velcro

JROTC Velcro nametape

Combat Boot hot weather, or Combat Boot temperate weather

Velcro backed rank insignia

Wear of the ACU Coat / Trousers

- The coat is worn hook and looped and zipped.
- The coat has a hook and loop fasteners for wearing shoulder sleeve insignia, rank, JROTC patch, and school name tape.
- The mandarin collar will be normally worn in the down position.
- Cadets are authorized to wear the mandarin collar in the up position when weather conditions dictate the wear as prescribed by the SAI/AI.
- The coat is normally worn outside the trousers, and the trousers are worn with a belt. The coat may also be worn inside the trousers when directed by the SAI/AI. The coat will not extend below the top of the cargo pocket on the trousers and will not be higher than the bottom of the side pocket on the trousers.
- The elbow pouch with hook and loop closure for internal elbow pad inserts must be closed at all times.
- Sleeves will be worn down at all times, and not rolled or cuffed.
- The moisture wicking tan t-shirt or cotton t-shirt is worn underneath the coat and it is tucked inside the trousers at all times.
- Cadets will wear the trousers tucked into the top of the boots or bloused using the draw strings at the bottom of the trousers . When bloused, the trousers should not extend below the third eyelet from the top of the boot.
- The ACU is meant to fit loosely and comfortably. Alterations to hinder this is not authorized.
- Cadets will wear the ACU in accordance with CCR 145-2.
- Cadets will not wrap the trouser leg around the leg tightly enough to present a pegged appearance or insert any items inside the trouser leg to create a round appearance at the bottom of the trouser leg.

Wear of the ACU Headgear

- The ACU Patrol Cap will be the only headgear worn with the uniform.
- Cadets will wear the ACU Patrol Cap straight on the head so that the cap band creates a straight line around the head, parallel to the ground.
- The Patrol Cap will fit snugly and comfortably around the largest part of the head without distortion or excessive gaps. The cap is worn so that no hair is visible on the forehead beneath the cap. Sewn or pin on rank is worn on the ACU Patrol Cap.
- The Velcro area on the rear of the cap will remain blank at all times.

Wear of Desert / Optional Boots

- Black boots are NOT authorized for wear with the ACU.
- Army Combat Boots – (Hot Weather and temperate weather) made of tan rough side out cattle hide leather with a plain toe and tan rubber outsoles.
- The boots are laced diagonally with tan laces, with excess lace tucked into the top of the boot under the bloused trousers, or wrapped around the top side of the boot.
- Only boots with tan rubber outsoles are authorized for wear .

The ACU Care Policy

- Wash in cold water and mild detergent containing no optical brighteners or bleach. Tumble dry at low heat (not to exceed 130 degrees Fahrenheit).
- Remove immediately from the dryer and fold flat or place on a rustproof hanger to ensure heat from the dryer does not set wrinkles.
- To drip dry, remove from the washer/water and place on a rustproof hanger. Do not wring or twist. "

...DO NOT STARCH THE ARMY COMBAT UNIFORM UNDER ANY CIRCUMSTANCES. THE USE OF STARCH, SIZING, AND ANY PROCESS THAT INVOLVES DRY-CLEANING OR A STEAM PRESS WILL ADVERSELY AFFECT THE TREATMENTS AND DURABILITY OF THE UNIFORM AND IS NOT AUTHORIZED"

ACU MILPER MESSAGE, AMENDMENT TO AR 670-1

Unit 1: Citizenship in Action
Chapter 1: Foundations of Army JROTC and Getting Involved
Lesson 6: The Stars and Stripes

DISPLAY OF THE FLAG

PLEDGE OF ALLEGIANCE

"I pledge allegiance to the flag of the United States of America and to the Republic for which it stands, one Nation under God, indivisible, with liberty and justice for all."

How to Fold the Flag

Step 1

To properly fold the flag, begin by holding it waist-high with another person so that its surface is parallel to the ground.

Step 2

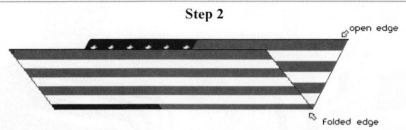

Fold the lower half of the stripe section lengthwise **over** the field of stars, holding the bottom and top edges securely.

Step 3

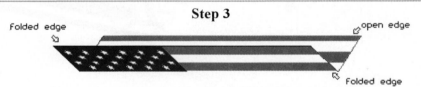

Fold the flag **again** lengthwise with the blue field on the **outside**.

Step 4

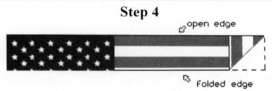

Make a triangular fold by bringing the striped corner of the folded edge to meet the open (top) edge of the flag.

Step 5

Turn the outer (end) point inward, parallel to the open edge, to form a second triangle.

Step 6

The triangular folding is continued until the entire length of the flag is folded in this manner.

Step 7

When the flag is completely folded, only a triangular blue field of stars should be visible.

The Star-Spangled Banner

O say, can you see, by the dawn's early light,
What so proudly we hailed at the twilight's last gleaming,
Whose broad stripes and bright stars, through the perilous fight,
O'er the ramparts we watched were so gallantly streaming?
And the rockets' red glare, the bombs bursting in air
Gave proof through the night that our flag was still there,
O say, does that Star-Spangled Banner yet wave
O'er the land of the free and the home of the brave?

On the shore dimly seen through the mist of the deep,
Where the foe's haughty host in dread silence reposes,
What is that which the breeze, o'er the towering steep
As it fitfully blows, half conceals, half discloses?
Now it catches the gleam of the morning's first beam,
In full glory reflected now shines on the stream;
'Til the Star-Spangled Banner--O long may it wave
O'er the land of the free and the home of the brave.

O thus be it ever when free men shall stand
Between their loved homes and the war's desolation;
Blest with victory and peace, may the heaven rescued land
Praise the Power that has made and preserved us a nation.
Then conquer we must, when our cause it is just,
And this be our motto, "In God is our trust;"
And the Star-Spangled Banner in triumph shall wave
O'er the land of the free and the home of the brave.

Unit 1: Citizenship in Action
Chapter 1: Foundations of Army JROTC and Getting Involved
Lesson 8: American Military Traditions, Customs, and Courtesies

<u>Title</u>	<u>*How to Address*</u>
All general officers	*"General"*
Colonels and Lieutenant Colonels	*"Colonel"*
Majors	*"Major"*
Captains	*"Captain"*
Lieutenants	*"Lieutenant"*
Chaplains	*"Chaplain"*
Cadets	*"Mister," "Miss" or "Cadet"*
Officer Candidates	*"Candidate"*
Warrant Officers	*"Mister" or "Miss"*
Sergeant Major	*"Sergeant Major"*
First Sergeants	*"First Sergeant"*
All other Sergeants	*"Sergeant"*
Corporals	*"Corporal"*
All specialists	*"Specialist"*
Privates and privates first class	*"Private"*

Unit 1: Citizenship in Action
Chapter 1: Foundations of Army JROTC and Getting Involved
Lesson 9: Basic Command and Staff Principles

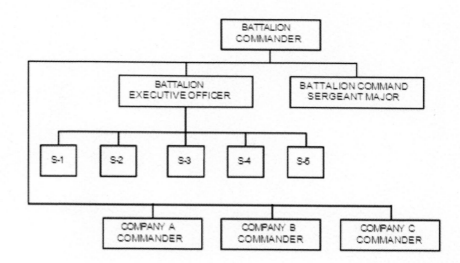

Unit 1: Citizenship in Action
Chapter 2: Service to the Nation
Lesson 1: The Department of Defense

CHAIN OF COMMAND

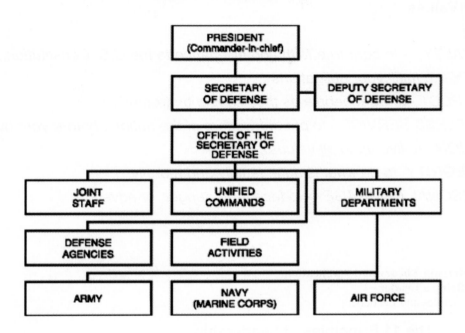

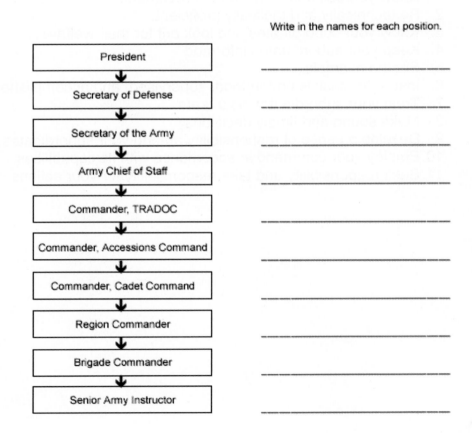

Write in the names for each position.

Unit 2: Leadership Theory and Application
Chapter 1: Being a Leader
Lesson 3: Leadership from the Inside Out

Army Values

L *OYALTY - to bear true faith and allegiance to the U.S. Constitution...your peers*

D *UTY - to fulfill your obligations*

R *ESPECT - to treat people as they should be treated*

S *ELFLESS SERVICE - to put the welfare of the nation...before your own*

H *ONOR - to live up to <u>all</u> values*

I *NTEGRITY- to do what is right, legally and morally*

P *ERSONAL COURAGE - to face fear, danger, or adversity*

Unit 2: Leadership Theory and Application
Chapter 1: Being a Leader
Lesson 4: Principles and Leadership

The 11 Principles of Leadership

1. Know yourself and seek self-improvement.
2. Be technically and tactically proficient.
3. Know your subordinates and look out for their welfare.
4. Keep your subordinates informed.
5. Set the example.
6. Insure the task is understood, supervised, and accomplished.
7. Train your subordinates as a team.
8. Make sound and timely decisions.
9. Develop a sense of responsibility among your subordinates.
10. Employ your command in accordance with its capabilities.
11. Seek responsibility and take responsibility for your actions.

Unit 2: Leadership Theory and Application
Chapter 2: Leadership Skills
Lesson 4: Stationary Movements

Position of Attention:

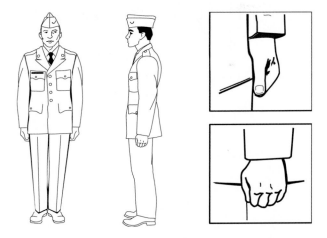

Parade Rest:

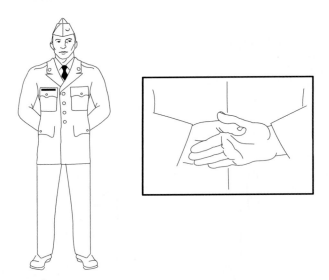

Facing Right or Left:

About Face:

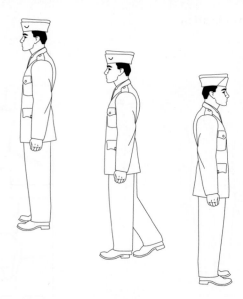

(Refer to FM 22-5, dtd 1986, for all executions of drill or stationary movements.)

Unit 2: Leadership Theory and Application
Chapter 2: Leadership Skills
Lesson 5: Steps and Marching

30-inch Step:

15-inch Step:

Unit 2: Leadership Theory and Application
Chapter 2: Leadership Skills
Lesson 6: Squad Drill

Squad Formations

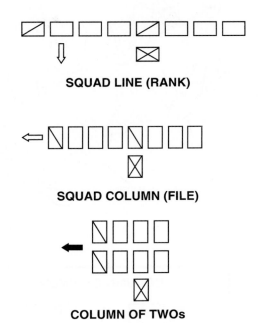

SQUAD LINE (RANK)

SQUAD COLUMN (FILE)

COLUMN OF TWOs

Normal Intervals:

Close Intervals:

Changing Direction:

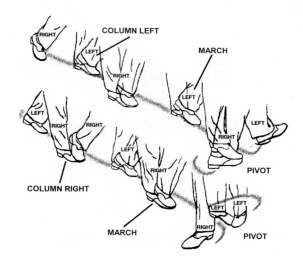

Column of Twos:

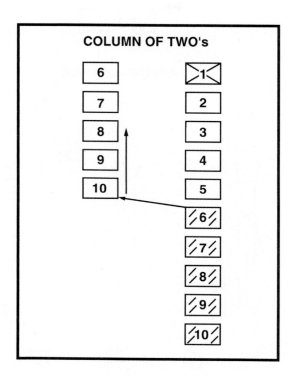

Unit 2: Leadership Theory and Application
Chapter 4: Leadership Strategies
Lesson 2: Performance Indicators

Performance Indicators

Leaders of character and competence..			act to achieve excellence by providing purpose, direction and motivation.		
Values *"Be"*	**Attributes** *"Be"*	**Skills**[4] *"Know"*	**Actions**[5] *"Do"*		
			Influencing	**Operating**	**Improving**
Loyalty	Mental[1]	Interpersonal			
Duty			Communicating	Planning/ Preparing	Developing
Respect	Physical[2]	Conceptual			
Selfless Service			Decision Making	Executing	Building
Honor		Technical			
Integrity	Emotional[3]		Motivating	Assessing	Learning
Personal Courage		Tactical			

1 The mental attributes of an Army leader are will, self-discipline, initiative, judgment, self-confidence, intelligence, and cultural awareness.
2 The physical attributes of an Army leader are health fitness, physical fitness, and military and professional bearing.
3 The emotional attributes of an Army leader are self-control, balance, and stability.
4 The interpersonal, conceptual, technical, and tactical skills are different for direct, organizational, and strategic leaders.
5 The influencing, operating, and improving actions are different for direct, organizational, and strategic leaders.

Unit 2: Leadership Theory and Application
Chapter 4: Leadership Strategies
Lesson 4: Decision Making and Problem Solving

Seven Step Problem-Solving Process

Seven Step Problem-Solving Process

1. Identify the problem (recognize/define)

2. Gather information (facts/assumptions)

3. Develop courses of action (solutions)

4. Analyze and compare courses of action (alternatives/solutions)

5. Make a decision; select the best course of action (solution)

6. Make a plan

7. Implement the plan (assess the results)

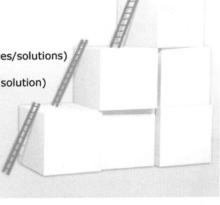

The QBOL Decision-Making Process

The 3Rs of Good Decision Making

1. They need to be RIGHT (based on law, ethics, and morals)

2. They need to be REALITY BASED (evidence supported as a RIGHT thing to do)

3. They need to be RESPONSIBLE (approved by society's most respected people)

Good decisions are not likely to present dangerous and high risk outcomes to those impacted by the action(s) taken.

Three Step Decision-Making Process

Step 1: Understanding the Problem

- Review the issue again.
- Write down what you know.
- Look for key phrases.
- Find the important information.
- Tell it in your own words.
- Tell what you are trying to find.

Step 2: Selecting Strategies

- Make a model – involve the senses.
- Make an organized list or table.
- Look for a pattern – find relationships.
- Guess (or conjecture) and test.
- Make an organized drawing or sketch.
- Work backwards – start with the consequence.
- Role-play – become an active player.
- Solve a simpler matter – try simulations.
- Use estimation.

Step 3: Looking Back: Checking the Answer

- Does the answer make sense?
- Is it reasonable?
- Can the issue be generalized?
- Is there a pattern?
- Are there other similar situations?

The Decision Making Process

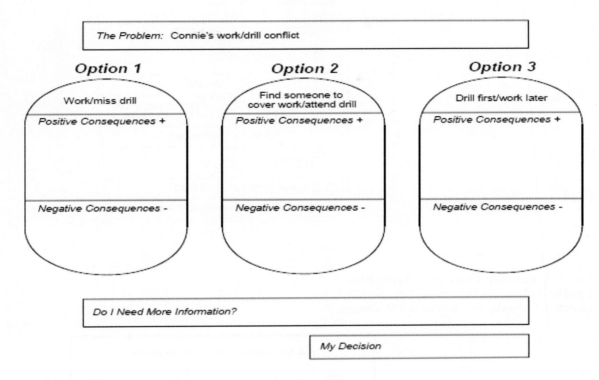

The Problem: Connie's work/drill conflict

Option 1	Option 2	Option 3
Work/miss drill	Find someone to cover work/attend drill	Drill first/work later

Positive Consequences +

Negative Consequences -

Do I Need More Information?

My Decision

Unit 2: Leadership Theory and Application
Chapter 5: Leading Others
Lesson 1: Platoon Drill

Platoon Formations:

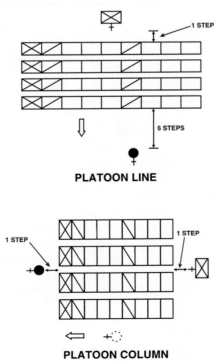

PLATOON LINE

PLATOON COLUMN

Counter Column March:

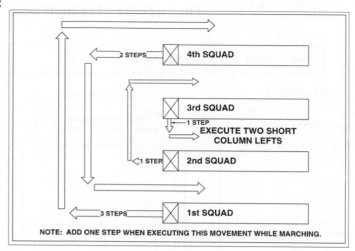

Unit 2: Leadership Theory and Application
Chapter 5: Leading Others
Lesson 3: Company Formations and Movement

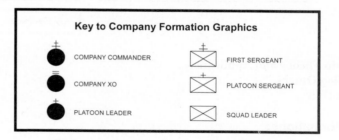

Company Formations:

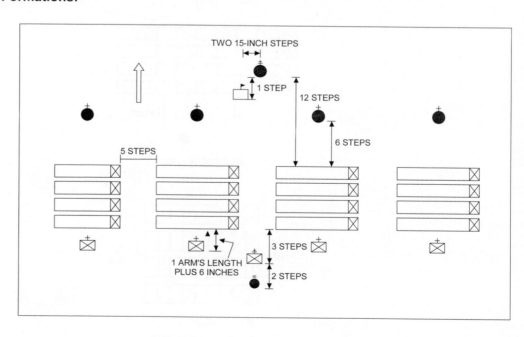

Company in Columns with Platoon in Columns:

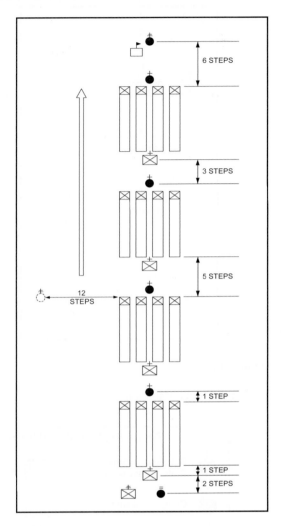

Forming a Company Mass:

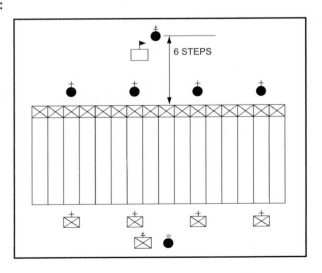

Company in Column with Platoons in Line:

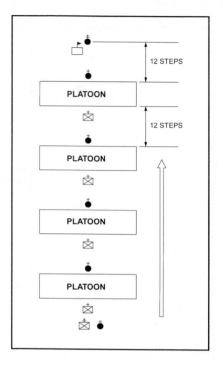

Unit 2: Leadership Theory and Application
Chapter 5: Leading Others
Lesson 4: Forming, Inspection, and Dismissing the Battalion

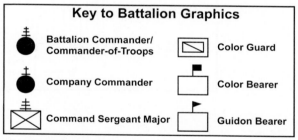

Battalion in Line with Companies in Line or Mass

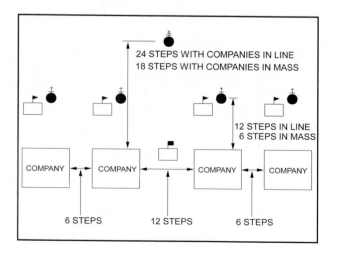

Battalion in Column with Companies in Column or Mass

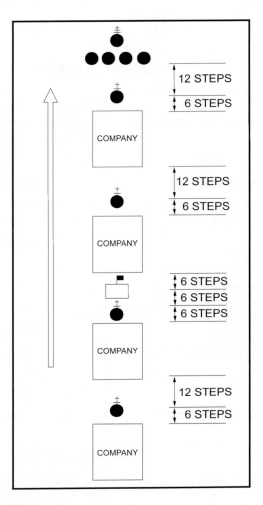

Battalion in Mass Formations:

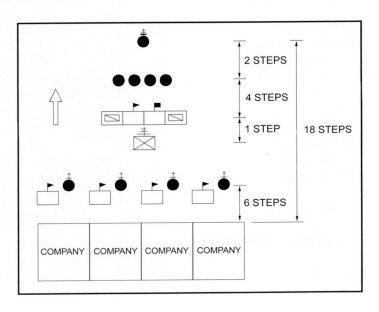

WINNING COLORS®

Builder Behaviors (brown, decide)

Builder Vocabulary:

Always Leading People
Power
Responsible
Duty
Results
Tradition
Money
Prepared
I Give Directions
Do It My Way
I Like To Get Things Done Now

Hot Buttons:

Down-to-earth and traditional

Planner Behaviors (green, think)

Planner Vocabulary:

Changing and Improving
Analyzing
Being My Best
Dreaming
Caring
Invention
Planning
Inner Life
Exactness
Seeks the Future
Freedom of Thought

Hot Buttons:

Freedom to think, dream, create

Adventurer Behaviors (red, act)

Adventurer Vocabulary:

Excitement
Test The Limits
Risk
Act and Perform
Fun
Action
Fast Machines
Freedom
Challenge
Do It Now!

Hot Buttons:

A life of fun, action and freedom

Relater Behaviors (blue, feel)

Relater Vocabulary:

We Are The World
Friendly
Romantic
I See Everything
Hugs Are Special
Giving
Teamwork
Groups
Wanting People to Like Me
Let's Get Along With Each Other

Hot Buttons:

Friendly, caring, feeling people

Unit 3: Foundations for Success
Chapter 1: Know Yourself - Socrates
Lesson 5: Pathways to Success (QBOL)

Stepping Stones to Success Self-Assessment

STEPPING STONE ONE: DREAMS AND GOALS
Dreams are creations of the mind. They represent our wishes for the future. When dreams inspire us, they become a gateway to possibility and reality. Goals focus on the specifics of what we want. Goals turn dreams into reality.

1.	You state (verbal/written) the definitions for dreams and goals
2.	You state the similarities and differences between dreams and goals
3.	You explain how dreams and goals contribute to your success
4.	You explain how to turn dreams into goals

STEPPING STONE TWO: SELF-ESTEEM (RESOURCE REVIEW)
Successful people have confidence in themselves (self-esteem). They have some of the resources (information, skills, books, equipment, etc.) they will need to gain forward movement in the direction of their goal.

5.	You state (verbal/written) the definition of self-esteem
6.	You explain how self-esteem contributes to success
7.	You conduct a personal resource review
8.	You explain how using your personal and environmental resources contribute to goal attainment

STEPPING STONE THREE: TEAM SUPPORT
Successful people surround themselves with people on whom they can rely for support, guidance, and direction in pursuit of their goals. They understand that achieving success in anything they do is rarely achieved in isolation.

9.	You state (verbal/written) the definition for team support
10.	You explain how team support contributes to success
11.	You give examples of strategies you can use to develop team support

STEPPING STONE FOUR: DECIDE AND PLAN
Successful people **decide** what they need to do and then make a **plan** they can follow to achieve their goal.

12.	You state (verbal/written) the definitions for decide and plan
13.	You explain (verbal/written) how decide and plan processes work together to achieve success
14.	You use decide and plan processes in a classroom experience

STEPPING STONE FIVE: POSITIVE MENTAL ATTITUDE
Successful people are positive, focused, and never give up on themselves or their goal. They may alter their goal, take more time to complete it than planned, or not complete their goal in its entirety, but do what they can given the challenges before them. Successful people are reality oriented in their thinking and know they will face setbacks, obstacles, challenges, and other potential Quarterbacks of Life Student Mentoring Program's Success Stoppers. They also realize that with patience, persistence, and a plan, most Quarterbacks of Life Student Mentoring Program's Success Stoppers can be overcome.

15.	You state (verbal/written) the definition for positive mental attitude (PMA)
16.	You explain (verbal/written) how having PMA contributes to achieving success
17.	You name a variety of PMA strategies that support achieving success
18.	You practice using PMA strategies

Unit 3: Foundations for Success
Chapter 2: Learning to Learn
Lesson 1: Brain Structure and Function

Triune Brain

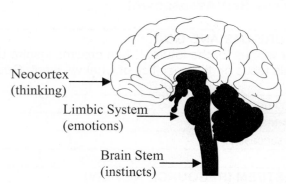

Neocortex
(thinking)

Limbic System
(emotions)

Brain Stem
(instincts)

The ***Neocortex*** is responsible for thinking and speaking. When activated by positive emotions, whole-brain activation can take place allowing high-level learning. The ***Limbic System*** is responsible for group interaction and emotions. It monitors fear, threat, intimidation, and put-downs and codes incoming information with positive or negative emotions. The ***Brain Stem***, also known as the Reptilian Brain, Reactive Complex and R-complex, governs primitive needs such as a sense of safety and survival. When the Limbic System detects fear, threats, intimidation, or put-downs, the R-complex takes over and downshifting occurs preventing high-level learning.

Brain Structure and Function

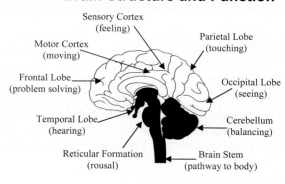

Sensory Cortex
(feeling)

Motor Cortex
(moving)

Parietal Lobe
(touching)

Frontal Lobe
(problem solving)

Occipital Lobe
(seeing)

Temporal Lobe
(hearing)

Cerebellum
(balancing)

Reticular Formation
(rousal)

Brain Stem
(pathway to body)

Unit 3: Foundations for Success
Chapter 2: Learning to Learn
Lesson 2: Left-Brain/Right-Brain

The Left/Right Brain hemisphere theory of Roger Sperry, suggests there are "two modes of thinking, verbal and nonverbal represented rather separately in left and right hemispheres" of the human brain. The left hemisphere tends to be verbal and analytic, while the right is nonverbal and global.

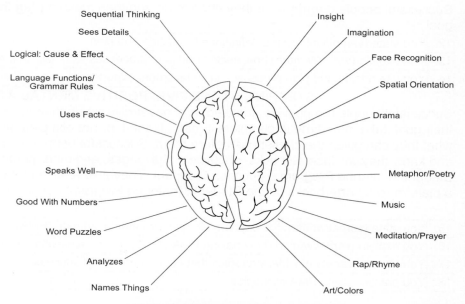

Sequential Thinking

Sees Details

Logical: Cause & Effect

Language Functions/
Grammar Rules

Uses Facts

Speaks Well

Good With Numbers

Word Puzzles

Analyzes

Names Things

Insight

Imagination

Face Recognition

Spatial Orientation

Drama

Metaphor/Poetry

Music

Meditation/Prayer

Rap/Rhyme

Art/Colors

LEFT-BRAIN/RIGHT-BRAIN FUNCTIONS

The Tiger Part of Me:
I Like Action!
Adventurer Behavioral Strengths

Words that describe me: Play, Perform, Take Chances, Fast Machines, Do It Now, Learn By Doing, Fun, Tell Jokes.

Communication Keys: Freedom of Action, Spur of the Moment, Challenge, Pushing the Limits, Excitement, Act it Out.

The Bull and Bear Part of Me:
I Like Leading!
Builder Behavioral Strengths

© 2004 Stefan

Words that describe me: Results, Traditional, Responsible, Productive, Control, Decisive, Leadership, Give Directions.

Communication keys: Bottom-Line, Awards, Rules, Respect, Power, Obedience, First is Important.

The Fox Part of Me:
I Like Thinking!
Planner Behavioral Strengths

© 2004 Stefan

Words that describe me: Imaginative, Perfectionist, Analytical, Thinker, Dreamer, Logical, New Ideas, Independent.

Communication Keys: Individual Freedom, Understand, Budget, Improve, Mystery, New Ways, Creative.

The Dolphin Part of Me:
I Like Being Part of a Team!
Relater Behavioral Strengths

© 2004 Stefan

Words that describe me: Team Builder, Sympathetic, Concern for Others, Want People to Like Me, Like to Talk.

Communication Keys: Personal Interaction, Friendly, Honest, Work Together, Respect for Feelings, Romantic, Want Harmony.

My Builder Behavioral Strengths

If I emphasize the **Bull and Bear Part of Me (brown),** I usually enjoy leading and being "up front" with people. I express myself openly and directly. I prefer taking a leadership role in a group or situation. I know what I ought to do and do not hesitate to remind other people about their responsibilities and commitments. I want status, recognition and power. I have a deep respect for traditions. I strive to be leader of any group. I believe in preparing and saving, thus building life on a rock-solid foundation, which will stand when the winds and rains come. I am a strong-willed, organized person who stands as a fortress for all to see, desiring respect and appreciation for the ways I help others to be their best.

Bull and Bear Vocabulary includes the following, in addition to those on the front of this card:

◆ results ◆ control ◆ at one's command ◆ reliable ◆
◆ law abiding ◆ duty ◆ dependable ◆ obedient ◆ organized ◆
◆ builder ◆ prepared ◆ accountable ◆ clear-cut ◆

People who show these behaviors in public: Condoleezza Rice (Planner Behaviors also), Bill O'Reilly (all four strengths), Frankie (Shark Tale) Secretary of State Hillary Clinton (all four strengths), General Collin Powell (all four strengths), President George W. Bush, The Lion King, Buffy the Vampire Slayer, General George Patton, President Ronald Reagan, Luch (Peanuts), Susie (Rugrat), Head Master Dumbledore (also a Planner), Banking Industry, Queen Elizabeth, Germany (as a country), U.S.A. (all four strengths), I.R.S. and the "Star Spangled Banner" (song).

Financial and personal success is not an accident!

Created by Stefan Neilson, MA.   Illustration: Mark Bezenar

Contact us for:

◆ Train-the-Trainer ◆ Keynotes ◆ Character Education ◆
◆ Seminars ◆ Violence Prevention ◆ Career Selection ◆
◆ Videos ◆ Leadership/Team Building ◆ Communication ◆

© 2007 Stefan   Financial and Personal Success, Inc.
P.O. Box 96, Mountlake Terrace, WA 98043
(425) 672 8222

winningcolors@mindspring.com
web sites: winningcolors.com & financialsuccessinc.com

Value at least $ 1,000,000.00. Your investment $ 10.00

My Adventurer Behavioral Strengths

If I emphasize the **Tiger Part of Me (red),** I just do it. I usually enjoy being where the action is and bring the fun and thrills into the routine of daily life. I am the entrepreneur and enjoy the excitement of taking chances. In times of crisis, I am at my best! I believe that people are free and make no bones about enjoying life without being bound by rules and regulations. I want excitement! I believe that money should be spent freely. The present moment is most important. Yesterday is easily forgotten and tomorrow is not relevant. Fast machines are an important part of my action world. I have fun flying over the rainbow rather than finding the pot of gold at the end. I am a free-spirited person for the entire world to see.

Tiger Vocabulary includes the following, in addition to those on the front of this card:

◆ thrill ◆ perform ◆ climb to the top ◆ games ◆ light-hearted ◆
◆ buy and sell ◆ stir the blood ◆ gamble ◆
◆ Shop 'til I drop ◆ fast machines ◆ good time ◆ danger ◆

These behaviors are exhibited in public by: General Colin Powell (all four behaviors), President Bill Clinton, Eddie Murphy, Michael Jordan (also a blue), Lil Bow-Wow, Marion Jones, Jackie Chan, Arnold Schwarzenegger, Robin Williams, Madonna, Ricky Martin, Richard Dean Anderson (Stargate SG1), Whoopi Goldberg, Garth Brooks, Elvis Presley, Jim Carrey, Michael Andretti, Tiger Woods (also a blue), Backstreet Boys, Bart Simpson, Angelica (Rugrat), Fred and George Wessley, Hagrid, 'N Sync, The Road Runner, Sponge Bob Square Pants, Oscar (Shark Tale), Australia (as a country), U.S.A. (all four strengths), and "Foot Loose" (song).

Created by Stefan Neilson, MA.   Illustration: Mark Bezenar

Contact us for:

◆ Train-the-Trainer ◆ Keynotes ◆
◆ Seminars ◆ Violence Prevention ◆ Career Selection ◆
◆ Videos ◆ Leadership/Team Building ◆ Communication ◆

© 2007 Stefan   Financial and Personal Success, Inc.
P.O. Box 96, Mountlake Terrace, WA 98043
(425) 672 8222

winningcolors@mindspring.com
web sites: winningcolors.com & financialsuccessinc.com

Value at least $ 1,000,000.00. Your investment $ 10.00

My Relater Behavioral Strengths

If I emphasize the **Dolphin Part of Me (blue),** I usually enjoy being with people and have a high regard for emotions. I am the team builder, the basic ingredient for success. I know that feelings are very important and will bend my needs to those of others. People are the most important part of my decision making. I like to work in a team. I want unity with others, am a romantic at heart and a sympathetic person by nature. I want opportunities to communicate and socialize with others. I believe that care and consideration are the rock-solid foundation of a successful and prosperous life. I have strong emotions, based on honesty and sincerity. I feel that I can help others become productive and happy.

Dolphin Vocabulary includes the following, in addition to those on the front of this card:

◆ team building ◆ harmony ◆ sympathy ◆ sharing ◆
◆ group projects ◆ brotherly love ◆
◆ concern for people ◆ honesty with others ◆ friendly ◆

People who show these behaviors in public: General Colin Powell (all four strengths), Oprah Winfrey, Bill Cosby, Billy Graham, President Jimmy Carter, Celine Dion, Rosie O'Donnell, Michael Jordan (also a red), Reba McEntire, Ronald McDonald (McDonald's), Snoopy, Chuckie (Rugrat), Lenny (Shar Tale), Mexico (as a country), Italy (as a country), U.S.A. (all four strengths(and "We are the World" (song).

Financial and personal success is not an accident!

Created by Stefan Neilson, MA.   Illustration: Mark Bezenar

Contact us for: ◆ Train-the-Trainer ◆ Keynotes ◆
◆ Seminars ◆ Violence Prevention ◆ Career Identification ◆
◆ Videos ◆ Leadership/Team Building ◆ Communication ◆

Financial and Personal Success, Inc.   © 2007 Stefan
P.O. Box 96, Mountlake Terrace, WA 98043
(425) 672 8222

winningcolors@mindspring.com
web sites: winningcolors.com & financialsuccessinc.com

Value at least $ 1,000,000.00. Your investment $ 10.00

My Planner Behavioral Strengths

If I emphasize the **Fox Part of Me (green),** I usually enjoy thinking about new and better ways for creating and doing things. I know that underlying details are important. I make sure that everything is brought into consideration before making an important decision. I want know-how. I want to do things right. I want to know new things. I am a thinker by nature. I believe in using time and money wisely. I am curious about the inner world of people. I want to understand nature. I am a creative person of reason and wisdom. I desire the ability to prepare for the future so that society might not only survive but also prosper.

Fox Vocabulary includes the following, in addition to those on the front of this card:

◆ magic ◆ intuitive ◆ imaginative ◆ cautious ◆
◆ dreamer ◆ creative ◆ new and better ways ◆
◆ theoretical ◆ science fiction ◆

(all four strengths), Laura Bush, Steven Spielberg, Prince William, Alexander G. Bell, President John F. Kennedy, Bill Gates, Gloria Estevan, Thomas Edison, Marge Simpson, James Earl Jones, Dr. Martin Luther King, Jr., Noriyuki Morita, Harry Potter, Hermione, Canada (as a country), France (as a country), U.S.A. (all four strengths) and "The Impossible Dream" (song).

Financial and personal success is not an accident!

Created by Stefan Neilson, MA.   Illustration: Mark Bezenar

Contact us for:

◆ Train-the-Trainer ◆ Keynotes ◆ Character Education ◆
◆ Seminars ◆ Violence Prevention ◆ Career Selection ◆
◆ Videos ◆ Leadership/Team Building ◆ Communication ◆

© 2007 Stefan   Financial and Personal Success, Inc.
P.O. Box 96, Mountlake Terrace, WA 98043
(425) 672 8222

winningcolors@mindspring.com
web sites: winningcolors.com & financialsuccessinc.com

Value at least $ 1,000,000.00. Your investment $ 10.00

Unit 3: Foundations for Success
Chapter 5: Conflict Resolution
Lesson 1: Causes of Conflict

Six Steps for Resolving Conflict

Unit 3: Foundations for Success
Chapter 8: Making a Difference with Service Learning
Lesson 1: Orientation to Service Learning

Orientation and Training
+ Meaningful Service
+ Structured Reflection
_____

SERVICE LEARNING

Unit 3: Foundations for Success
Chapter 8: Making a Difference with Service Learning
Lesson 2: Plan and Train for Your Exploratory Project

SERVICE LEARNING STEPS

1. Complete a pre-assessment of skill level using the Personal Skills Map from the JROTC Success Profiler.
2. Determine a school, community, or national need you can fill relating to class curriculum.
3. Brainstorm and select a meaningful service project that meets proposed guidelines.
4. Start learning log to record new knowledge, thoughts and feelings throughout all phases.
5. Plan and organize details of the service activity and discuss expectations.
6. Participate in a meaningful service activity that meets the service learning guidelines (Form 219-R).
7. Discuss and reflect on what you experienced (observation).
8. Discuss and reflect on what you gained from the experience (analysis).
9. Discuss and reflect on what you can do with the new information (integration).
10. Complete a project summary report, a final group evaluation form to judge teamwork, etc
11. Brief the experience to community members, administration, classmates, etc.
12. Complete a post-assessment using the personal skills map and related analysis to determine plan of action.

Sample Resume

Norma L. Cadet

394 N. Anywhere St. • Any Town, FL 24509 • 123.456.7890 • cadet@anytown.com

---

OBJECTIVE

To obtain a Graphic Designer position in the print/web industry utilizing creative and artistic talents.

EDUCATION

Sandy Beach High School, Cape Coral, FL

- Graduated in May 2010 with emphasis in art and business.
- Courses included: Computers, Typing, JROTC, Marketing, Public Speaking
- Honors Student, GPA: 3.5 on a 4.0 scale

EXPERIENCE

2009-2010 **PRINT WORKS STATIONARY**   Any Town, FL
Sales Representative

- Sold custom-printed stationary and print products.
- Organized computerized filing system to keep client base.
- Illustrated design ideas and custom logos for clientele.
- Designed web site for company and created a corporate image.
- Edited marketing video for company to send to corporate clients.

2008-2009 **GOLF & BEACH RESORT**   Any Town, FL
Lifeguard & Gift Shop Sales

- Completed Lifeguard Training and received certifications in CPR and First Aid.
- Worked cash register in the resort gift shop.

SKILLS

• Windows systems	• Macintosh systems	• Video Editing
• Illustration	• Color Management	• Animation
• HTML	• JavaScript	• 3-D Modeling

ACTIVITIES/SERVICE

• National Honors Society	• Army JROTC	• Swim Team
• Recycling Club	• Junior Achievement	• Student Council

References available upon request.

Unit 3: Foundations for Success
Chapter 10: Planning Skills and Social Responsibility
Lesson 1: Making the Right Choices

The F-I-N-D-S Decision-Making Model

1. **F**igure out the problem.

2. **I**dentify possible solutions.

3. **N**ame the pros and cons of each choice.

4. **D**ecide which is the best choice and then act on it.

5. **S**crutinize the decision.

Unit 3: Foundations for Success
Chapter 10: Planning Skills and Social Responsibility
Lesson 4: Cadet Etiquette Guide

Proper Place Setting

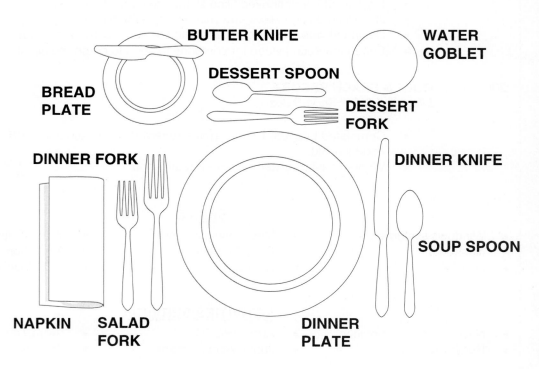

Unit 3: Foundations for Success
Chapter 12: Teaching Skills
Lesson 5: Thinking Maps® and Graphic Organizers

Thinking Maps®

Questions from Texts, Teachers and Tests	Thinking Processes	Thinking Maps as Tools
How are you defining this thing or idea? What is the context? What is your frame of reference?	**DEFINING IN CONTEXT**	Circle Map
How are you describing this thing? Which adjectives would best describe this thing?	**DESCRIBING QUALITIES**	Bubble Map
What are the similar and different qualities of these things? Which qualities do you value most? Why?	**COMPARING and CONTRASTING**	Double Bubble Map
What are the main ideas, supporting ideas, and details in this information?	**CLASSIFYING**	Tree Map
What are the component parts and subparts of this whole physical object?	**PART-WHOLE**	Brace Map
What happened? What is the sequence of events? What are the substages?	**SEQUENCING**	Flow Map
What are the causes and effects of this event? What might happen next?	**CAUSE and EFFECT**	Multi-Flow Map
What is the analogy being used? What is the guiding metaphor?	**SEEING ANALOGIES**	Bridge Map

1-9

Graphic Organizers

Concept Web

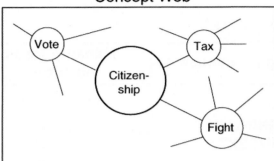

Mind Map

Ranking Ladder

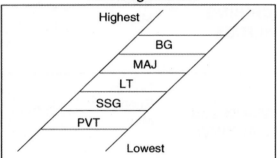

Venn Diagram

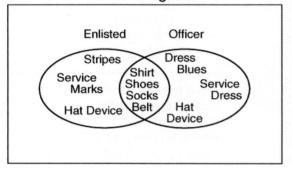

Double T-Chart

Before	During	After
Sleep	Work	Play
Study	Test	Relax

T-Chart

Poor Nutrition	
Problem	Solution
Eating junk food	Education

Sunshine Wheel

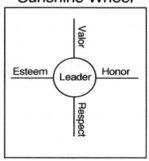

Looks-Sounds-Feels

Looks	Sounds	Feel
Shiny	Squeak	Smooth
New	Quiet	Worn

Pie Chart

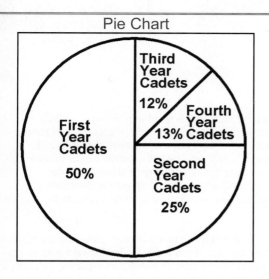

Fishbone

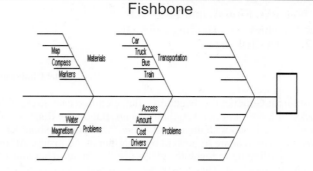

Matrix

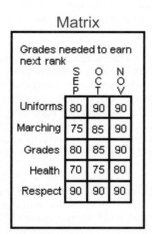

Analogy/Simile Chart

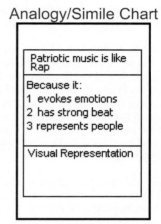

Sequence (Also known as Bridging Snapshots)

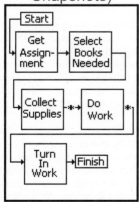

Unit 4: Wellness, Fitness, and First Aid
Chapter 1: Achieving a Healthy Lifestyle
Lesson 2: Cadet Challenge

Cadet Challenge

1. **Curl-ups:** Conduct this event on a flat, clean surface, preferably with a mat. Start cadets in a lying position on their backs with their knees up so their feet are flat on the floor and about 12 inches from their buttocks. Cadets should have their arms crossed with their hands placed on opposite shoulders and their elbows held close to the chest throughout the exercise. The feet are to be held by a partner at the instep. At the command "ready, go," cadets raise the trunks of their bodies, curling up to touch the elbows to the thighs. They must then lower their backs so that their shoulder blades touch the floor/mat. This constitutes one repetition of a curl-up. During each repetition, bouncing off the floor/mat is not allowed and the fingers must touch the shoulders at all times. Cadets must try to complete as many curl-ups as possible in 60 seconds.

2. **Partial Curl-ups**: This event should be used as an alternative to curl-ups. Have cadet lie on cushioned, clean surface with knees flexed and feet about 12 inches from buttocks. Do not hold or anchor the feet. Arms are extended forward with fingers resting on the legs and pointing toward the knees. The cadet's partner is behind the head with hands cupped under the cadet's head. The cadet being tested curls up slowly sliding the fingers up the legs until the fingertips touch the knees, then back down until the head touches the partner's hands. The curl-ups are done to a metronome (or audio tape, clapping, drums) with one complete curl-up every three seconds, and are continued until the cadet can do no more in rhythm (has not done the last three in rhythm) or has reached the target number for the test.

3. **Pull-ups:** Conduct this event using a horizontal bar approximately one and one-half inches in diameter. A doorway bar or a piece of pipe can serve the purpose. The bar should be high enough so that cadets can hang with their arms fully extended and their feet free of the floor/ground. Have cadets assume the hanging position on the bar using either an overhand grasp (palms facing away from body) or underhand grip (palms facing toward body). Cadets begin the exercise by first raising their body until the chin is over the bar without touching it. To complete one repetition, the body must be lowered to the full-hang starting position. During each repetition, the body must not swing; legs must not kick or bend, and the pull must not be jerky. Cadets are scored on the number of pull-ups they can correctly execute. There is no time limit on this event. For cadets who cannot accomplish one-pull-up, have them do the flexed-arm hang (below) as an alternative event.

4. **Flexed-arm Hang:** This event should be used when a cadet cannot execute one pull-up. (This event is only for the National Physical Fitness Award). Using a horizontal bar as in the pull-ups, have cadets climb a ladder until their chin is above the bar. They begin the exercise by grasping the bar with their hands, shoulder width apart -- using either an overhand grasp (palms facing away from body) or underhand grip (palms facing toward body. At the command "ready, go," the cadets step off the ladder. Simultaneously, an assistant instructor will remove the ladder and prevent any forward swinging of the legs. The cadet's chin should be level above the bar. Kicking and other body movements are not permitted while the cadets are on the bar. Start the stopwatch on the command "go" and stop it when the cadet's chin rests on the bar, the chin tilts backward to keep it above the bar, or the chin falls below the level of the bar. Scoring is to the nearest second

5. **Right Angle Push-ups:** The cadet lies face down on the mat in push-up position with hands under shoulders, fingers straight, and legs straight, parallel, and slightly apart, with the toes supporting the feet. The cadet straightens the arms, keeping the back and knees straight, then lowers the body until there is a 90-degree angle at the elbows, with the upper arms parallel to the floor. A partner holds her / his hand at the point of the 90-degree angle so that the cadet being tested goes down only until her / his shoulder touches the partner's hand, then back up. The push-ups are done to a metronome (or audio tape, clapping, drums) with one complete push-up every three seconds, and are continued until the cadet can do no more in rhythm (has not done the last three in rhythm) or has reached the target number for the PPFA.

6. **V-sit Reach:** Conduct this event on a flat, clean floor. Use a yardstick and adhesive tape to make a baseline that is two feet long. Make a measuring line perpendicular to the midpoint of the baseline extending two feet out from either side of the baseline. Place one-inch and half-inch marks along the measuring line with "0" where the baseline and measuring line intersect. Have cadets remove their shoes and sit on the floor with the soles of their feet placed immediately behind the baseline. The measuring line should be between their heels, which should be 8 to 12 inches apart. Cadets must clasp their thumbs so that their hands are together, palms down, and place them on the floor between their legs. While their legs are held flat on the floor by a partner (or partners), cadets performing the exercise keep the soles of their feet perpendicular to the floor (feet flexed) and slowly reach forward along the measuring line as far as possible keeping the fingers in contact with the floor. Cadets receive three practice tries for the v-sit reach. On the fourth extension, cadets must hold their farthest reach for three seconds. Scores are recorded where fingertips touch the floor to the nearest half inch. Scores beyond the baseline are recorded as plus scores, whereas those behind the baseline are recorded as minus scores.

7. **Sit and Reach:** A specially constructed box with a measuring scale marked in centimeters, with 23 centimeters at the level of the feet. Cadet removes shoes and sits on floor with knees fully extended, feet shoulder-width apart and soles of the feet held flat against the end of the box. With hands on top of each other, palms down, and legs held flat, cadet reaches along the measuring line as far as possible. After three practice reaches, the fourth reach is held while the distance is recorded. Participants are most flexible after a warm-up run. Best results may occur immediately after performing the endurance run. Legs must remain straight, soles of feet against box and fingertips of both hands should reach evenly along measuring line. Scores are recorded to the nearest centimeter.

8. **One-Mile Run/Walk:** Conduct this event on a flat area that has a known measured distance of one mile with a designated start and finish line. Give cadets a lightweight numbered device to carry or wear in any manner that will not slow them down while running. (Note: Use of the numbered device makes it possible to have many cadets run at one time by having them pair off before the start of the event, then having one cadet from each pair run while the other cadets keep track of the number of laps their partners complete as well as listening for their times as they cross the finish line.) Start cadets at the standing position. At the command "ready, go," start the cadets running the one-mile distance. Although walking is permitted, encourage cadets to cover the distance in the shortest time possible. Scoring should be to the nearest second.

9. **Shuttle Run:** Conduct this event on an area that has two parallel lines 30 feet apart. The width of a regulation volleyball court can serve as a suitable area. Start cadets at the standing position. At the command "ready, go," have the cadets run to the opposite line, pick up one block, run back to the starting line, and place the block behind the line. Cadets then run back and pick up the second block, which they carry across the line. Two runs are allowed for this event with the better of the runs recorded. Scoring should be to the nearest tenth of a second.

Awards for Completing the Cadet Challenge

- Cadets that successfully complete all events will receive a participation certificate signed by the Bde Cdr or a designated representative.

- The President's Physical Fitness Award recognizes students who achieve an outstanding level of physical fitness. Students who score at or above the 85th percentile on all events are eligible for this award. Awards may be requested by accessing the President's Challenge web site at http://www.presidentschallenge.org/educators/program_details.aspx.

- The JROTC Physical Fitness Ribbon (N-2-2) will be presented to cadets who receive the 85th percentile rating or better in each of the five events of the Cadet Challenge program.

- The National Physical Fitness Award recognizes students who demonstrate a basic, yet challenging level of physical fitness. Students who score above 50% percentile on all five events are eligible for this award.

- The JROTC Athletics Ribbon (N-2-3) will be presented to cadets who receive the 50th percentile rating or better in each of the five events of the Cadet Challenge program.

- The top five male and five female cadets in each unit will receive individual medals

The Presidential Physical Fitness Award Qualifying Standards

In order to qualify for this award, participants must achieve at least the 85th percentile in all 5 events represented below. These standards are based on the 1985 School Population Fitness Survey and validated in 1998, by means of comparison with a large nationwide sample collected in 1994.

	Age	Curl-Ups (# one minute)	Partial* Curl-Ups (#) OR	Shuttle Run (seconds)	V-Sit Reach (inches)	Sit and Reach (centimeters) OR	One-Mile Run (min:sec) OR	Distance Options** 1/4 mile (min:sec)	1/2 mile (min:sec)	Pull-Ups (#) OR	Rt. Angle Push-Ups (#)
BOYS	6	33	22	12.1	+3.5	31	10:15	1:55		2	9
	7	36	24	11.5	+3.5	30	9:22	1:48		4	14
	8	40	30	11.1	+3.0	31	8:48		3:30	5	17
	9	41	37	10.9	+3.0	31	8:31		3:30	5	18
	10	45	35	10.3	+4.0	30	7:57			6	22
	11	47	43	10.0	+4.0	31	7:32			6	27
	12	50	64	9.8	+4.0	31	7:11			7	31
	13	53	59	9.5	+3.5	33	6:50			7	39
	14	56	62	9.1	+4.5	36	6:26			10	40
	15	57	75	9.0	+5.0	37	6:20			11	42
	16	56	73	8.7	+6.0	38	6:08			11	44
	17	55	66	8.7	+7.0	41	6:06			13	53
GIRLS	6	32	22	12.4	+5.5	32	11:20	2:00		2	9
	7	34	24	12.1	+5.0	32	10:36	1:55		2	14
	8	38	30	11.8	+4.5	33	10:02		3:58	2	17
	9	39	37	11.1	+5.5	33	9:30		3:53	2	18
	10	40	33	10.8	+6.0	33	9:19			3	20
	11	42	43	10.5	+6.5	34	9:02			3	19
	12	45	50	10.4	+7.0	36	8:23			2	20
	13	46	59	10.2	+7.0	38	8:13			2	21
	14	47	48	10.1	+8.0	40	7:59			2	20
	15	48	38	10.0	+8.0	43	8:08			2	20
	16	45	49	10.1	+9.0	42	8:23			1	24
	17	44	58	10.0	+8.0	42	8:15			1	25

The National Physical Fitness Award Qualifying Standards

In order to qualify for this award, participants must achieve at least the 50th percentile in all 5 events represented below. These standards are based on the 1985 School Population Fitness Survey and validated in1998, by means of comparison with a large nationwide sample collected in 1994.

	Age	Curl-Ups (# one minute)	Partial* Curl-Ups (#) OR	Shuttle Run (seconds)	V-Sit Reach (inches)	Sit and Reach (centimeters) OR	One-Mile Run (min:sec) OR	Distance Options** 1/4 mile (min:sec)	1/2 mile (min:sec)	Pull-Ups (#) OR	Rt. Angle Push-Ups (#) OR	Flexed-Arm Hang (sec)
BOYS	6	22	10	13.3	+1.0	26	12:36	2:21		1	7	6
	7	28	13	12.8	+1.0	25	11:40	2:10		1	8	8
	8	31	17	12.2	+0.5	25	11:05		4:22	1	9	10
	9	32	20	11.9	+1.0	25	10:30		4:14	2	12	10
	10	35	24	11.5	+1.0	25	9:48			2	14	12
	11	37	26	11.1	+1.0	25	9:20			2	15	11
	12	40	32	10.6	+1.0	26	8:40			2	18	12
	13	42	39	10.2	+0.5	26	8:06			3	24	14
	14	45	40	9.9	+1.0	28	7:44			5	24	20
	15	45	45	9.7	+2.0	30	7:30			6	30	30
	16	45	37	9.4	+3.0	30	7:10			7	30	28
	17	44	42	9.4	+3.0	34	7:04			8	37	30
GIRLS	6	23	10	13.8	+2.5	27	13:12	2:26		1	6	5
	7	25	13	13.2	+2.0	27	12:56	2:21		1	8	6
	8	29	17	12.9	+2.0	28	12:30		4:56	1	9	8
	9	30	20	12.5	+2.0	28	11:52		4:50	1	12	8
	10	30	24	12.1	+3.0	28	11:22			1	13	8
	11	32	27	11.5	+3.0	29	11:17			1	11	7
	12	35	30	11.3	+3.5	30	11:05			1	10	7
	13	37	40	11.1	+3.5	31	10:23			1	11	8
	14	37	30	11.2	+4.5	33	10:06			1	10	9
	15	36	26	11.0	+5.0	36	9:58			1	15	7
	16	35	26	10.9	+5.5	34	10:31			1	12	7
	17	34	40	11.0	+4.5	35	10:22			1	16	7

*Norms from Canada Fitness Award Program, Health Canada, Government of Canada with permission. **Note: 1/4 and 1/2 mile norms from Amateur Athletic Union Physical Fitness Program with permission.

The Participant Physical Fitness Award Qualifying Standards

Those who attempt all five events, but have one or more scores fall below the 50th percentile (see chart above) are eligible for the Participant Award.

Unit 4: Wellness, Fitness, and First Aid
Chapter 1: Achieving a Healthy Lifestyle
Lesson 4: Nutrition - You Are What You Eat

TYPES OF NUTRIENTS

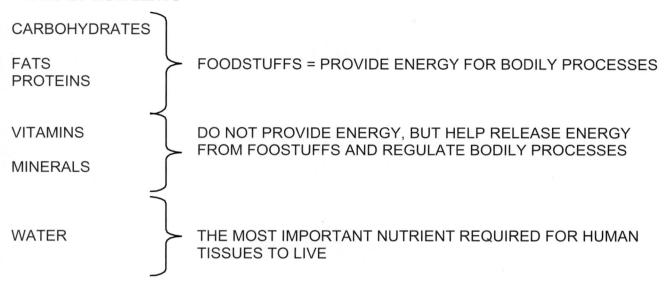

CARBOHYDRATES

FATS
PROTEINS

FOODSTUFFS = PROVIDE ENERGY FOR BODILY PROCESSES

VITAMINS

MINERALS

DO NOT PROVIDE ENERGY, BUT HELP RELEASE ENERGY FROM FOOSTUFFS AND REGULATE BODILY PROCESSES

WATER

THE MOST IMPORTANT NUTRIENT REQUIRED FOR HUMAN TISSUES TO LIVE

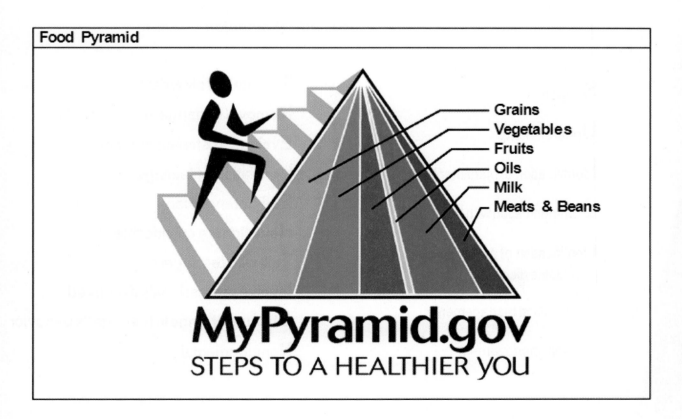

Food Pyramid

Grains
Vegetables
Fruits
Oils
Milk
Meats & Beans

MyPyramid.gov
STEPS TO A HEALTHIER YOU

Unit 4: Wellness, Fitness, and First Aid
Chapter 1: Achieving a Healthy Lifestyle
Lesson 5: At Risk - Suicide Awareness and Prevention

Signs of Suicide

Stress

Unsupported

Isolation

Calculated (intentional)

Impulsivity

Depression

Attempted previously

Low self-esteem

Suicide Prevention

Support

Understanding

Identification of plan/intent

Communication with teenagers

Identification of any underlying psychiatric disorder

Depression management

Esteem improvement

Parental involvement

Removal of dangerous materials

Evaluation after an attempt

Ventilation of feelings

Early intervention

Never ignore suicide threat

Talk with teenagers

Involve professionals if required

Observe change in teenager's behavior

Nonjudgmental

Unit 6: Citizenship and American History
Chapter 1: You the People – The Citizenship Skills
Lesson 1: The Preamble

The Preamble to the United States Constitution

We the people of the United States, in order to form a more perfect union, establish justice, insure domestic tranquility, provide for the common defense, promote the general welfare, and secure the blessing of liberty to ourselves and our prosperity, do ordain and establish this Constitution for the United States of America.

Unit 6: Citizenship and American History
Chapter 3: Creating the Constitution
Lesson 1: Articles of Confederation 1781

The Declaration of Independence

WHEN in the Course of human Events, it becomes necessary for one People to dissolve the Political Bands which have connected them with another, and to assume among the Powers of the Earth, the separate and equal Station to which the Laws of Nature and of Nature's God entitle them, a decent Respect to the Opinions of Mankind requires that they should declare the causes which impel them to the Separation.

WE hold these Truths to be self-evident, that all Men are created equal, that they are endowed by their Creator with certain unalienable Rights, that among these are Life, Liberty and the Pursuit of Happiness -- That to secure these Rights, Governments are instituted among Men, deriving their just Powers from the Consent of the Governed, that whenever any Form of Government becomes destructive of these Ends, it is the Right of the People to alter or to abolish it, and to institute new Government, laying its Foundation on such Principles, and organizing its Powers in such Form, as to them shall seem most likely to effect their Safety and Happiness. Prudence, indeed, will dictate that Governments long established should not be changed for light and transient Causes; and accordingly all Experience hath shewn, that Mankind are more disposed to suffer, while Evils are sufferable, than to right themselves by abolishing the Forms to which they are accustomed. But when a long Train of Abuses and Usurpations, pursuing invariably the same Object, evinces a Design to reduce them under absolute Despotism, it is their Right, it is their Duty, to throw off such Government, and to provide new Guards for their future Security. Such has been the patient Sufferance of these Colonies; and such is now the Necessity which constrains them to alter their former Systems of Government. The History of the present King of Great- Britain is a History of repeated Injuries and Usurpations, all having in direct Object the Establishment of an absolute Tyranny over these States. To prove this, let Facts be submitted to a candid World.

HE has refused his Assent to Laws, the most wholesome and necessary for the public Good.

HE has forbidden his Governors to pass Laws of immediate and pressing Importance, unless suspended in their Operation till his Assent should be obtained; and when so suspended, he has utterly neglected to attend to them.

HE has refused to pass other Laws for the Accommodation of large Districts of People, unless those People would relinquish the Right of Representation in the Legislature, a Right inestimable to them, and formidable to Tyrants only.

HE has called together Legislative Bodies at Places unusual, uncomfortable, and distant from the Depository of their public Records, for the sole Purpose of fatiguing them into Compliance with his Measures.

HE has dissolved Representative Houses repeatedly, for opposing with manly Firmness his Invasions on the Rights of the People.

HE has refused for a long Time, after such Dissolutions, to cause others to be elected; whereby the Legislative Powers, incapable of the Annihilation, have returned to the People at large for their exercise; the State remaining in the mean time exposed to all the Dangers of Invasion from without, and the Convulsions within.

HE has endeavoured to prevent the Population of these States; for that Purpose obstructing the Laws for Naturalization of Foreigners; refusing to pass others to encourage their Migrations hither, and raising the Conditions of new Appropriations of Lands.

HE has obstructed the Administration of Justice, by refusing his Assent to Laws for establishing Judiciary Powers.

HE has made Judges dependent on his Will alone, for the Tenure of their Offices, and the Amount and Payment of their Salaries.

HE has erected a Multitude of new Offices, and sent hither Swarms of Officers to harrass our People, and eat out their Substance.

HE has kept among us, in Times of Peace, Standing Armies, without the consent of our Legislatures.

HE has affected to render the Military independent of and superior to the Civil Power.

HE has combined with others to subject us to a Jurisdiction foreign to our Constitution, and unacknowledged by our Laws; giving his Assent to their Acts of pretended Legislation:

FOR quartering large Bodies of Armed Troops among us;

FOR protecting them, by a mock Trial, from Punishment for any Murders which they should commit on the Inhabitants of these States:

FOR cutting off our Trade with all Parts of the World:

FOR imposing Taxes on us without our Consent:

FOR depriving us, in many Cases, of the Benefits of Trial by Jury:

FOR transporting us beyond Seas to be tried for pretended Offences:

FOR abolishing the free System of English Laws in a neighbouring Province, establishing therein an arbitrary Government, and enlarging its Boundaries, so as to render it at once an Example and fit Instrument for introducing the same absolute Rules into these Colonies:

FOR taking away our Charters, abolishing our most valuable Laws, and altering fundamentally the Forms of our Governments:

FOR suspending our own Legislatures, and declaring themselves invested with Power to legislate for us in all Cases whatsoever.

HE has abdicated Government here, by declaring us out of his Protection and waging War against us.

HE has plundered our Seas, ravaged our Coasts, burnt our Towns, and destroyed the Lives of our People.

HE is, at this Time, transporting large Armies of foreign Mercenaries to compleat the Works of Death, Desolation, and Tyranny, already begun with circumstances of Cruelty and Perfidy, scarcely paralleled in the most barbarous Ages, and totally unworthy the Head of a civilized Nation.

HE has constrained our fellow Citizens taken Captive on the high Seas to bear Arms against their Country, to become the Executioners of their Friends and Brethren, or to fall themselves by their Hands.

HE has excited domestic Insurrections amongst us, and has endeavoured to bring on the Inhabitants of our Frontiers, the merciless Indian Savages, whose known Rule of Warfare, is an undistinguished Destruction, of all Ages, Sexes and Conditions.

IN every stage of these Oppressions we have Petitioned for Redress in the most humble Terms: Our repeated Petitions have been answered only by repeated Injury. A Prince, whose Character is thus marked by every act which may define a Tyrant, is unfit to be the Ruler of a free People.

NOR have we been wanting in Attentions to our British Brethren. We have warned them from Time to Time of Attempts by their Legislature to extend an unwarrantable Jurisdiction over us. We have reminded them of the Circumstances of our Emigration and Settlement here. We have appealed to their native Justice and Magnanimity, and we have conjured them by the Ties of our common Kindred to disavow these Usurpations, which, would inevitably interrupt our Connections and Correspondence. They too have been deaf to the Voice of Justice and of Consanguinity. We must, therefore, acquiesce in the Necessity, which denounces our Separation, and hold them, as we hold the rest of Mankind, Enemies in War, in Peace, Friends.

WE, therefore, the Representatives of the UNITED STATES OF AMERICA, in GENERAL CONGRESS, Assembled, appealing to the Supreme Judge of the World for the Rectitude of our Intentions, do, in the Name, and by Authority of the good People of these Colonies, solemnly Publish and Declare, That these United Colonies are, and of Right ought to be, FREE AND INDEPENDENT STATES; that they are absolved from all Allegiance to the British Crown, and that all political Connection between them and the State of Great-Britain, is and ought to be totally dissolved; and that as FREE AND INDEPENDENT STATES, they have full Power to levy War, conclude Peace, contract Alliances, establish Commerce, and to do all other Acts and Things which INDEPENDENT STATES may of right do. And for the support of this Declaration, with a firm Reliance on the Protection of divine Providence, we mutually pledge to each other our Lives, our Fortunes, and our sacred Honor.

John Hancock.
GEORGIA, Button Gwinnett, Lyman Hall, Geo. Walton.
NORTH-CAROLINA, Wm. Hooper, Joseph Hewes, John Penn.

SOUTH-CAROLINA, Edward Rutledge, Thos Heyward, junr., Thomas Lynch, junr., Arthur Middleton.

MARYLAND, Samuel Chase, Wm. Paca, Thos. Stone, Charles Carroll, of Carrollton.

VIRGINIA, George Wythe, Richard Henry Lee, Ths. Jefferson, Benja. Harrison, Thos. Nelson, jr., Francis Lightfoot Lee, Carter Braxton.

PENNSYLVANIA, Robt. Morris, Benjamin Rush, Benja. Franklin, John Morton, Geo. Clymer, Jas. Smith, Geo. Taylor, James Wilson, Geo. Ross.

DELAWARE, Caesar Rodney, Geo. Read.

NEW-YORK, Wm. Floyd, Phil. Livingston, Frank Lewis, Lewis Morris.

NEW-JERSEY, Richd. Stockton, Jno. Witherspoon, Fras. Hopkinson, John Hart, Abra. Clark.

NEW-HAMPSHIRE, Josiah Bartlett, Wm. Whipple, Matthew Thornton.

MASSACHUSETTS-BAY, Saml. Adams, John Adams, Robt. Treat Paine, Elbridge Gerry.

RHODE-ISLAND AND PROVIDENCE, C. Step. Hopkins, William Ellery.

CONNECTICUT, Roger Sherman, Saml. Huntington, Wm. Williams, Oliver Wolcott.

IN CONGRESS, JANUARY 18, 1777.

NOTES

NOTES